Garden of Values

Cultivating Values, A Nature-Inspired Way

Titus Yong
with Chloe Young
& Aeron Young

Garden of Values

Cultivating Values,
A Nature-Inspired Way

By Titus Yong

with Chloe Young & Aeron Young

ISBN 978-98-11-3631-3

First Edition
Printed in Singapore

Cover design and layout by Jia Lee

Please contact the authors at the following email:
hello@gardenofvalues.com

Dedicated to families
and learning teams.

With gratitude to an inspiring teacher,
Professor J. Richard Hackman (1940—2013),
who sparked my fascination for creative teams.

Introduction

What's the precious opportunity?

This is a story of our journey: to live fulfilling lives as a team & family.

This book recounts our struggles, joys and triumphs, and the lessons we have learnt. We made multiple journeys, took thousands of photos, researched on dozens of values, and debated on the choices of values to adopt. Our lessons have been compiled into a roadmap of sorts: a nature-inspired way we have taken and are still taking.

Many of us start off with good intentions. We want success in all areas of our lives: satisfying work, wonderful family and friends, healthy bodies & even healthier bank accounts, and an attainment of balance and harmony. Or at least a semblance of all these.

Yet the reality is that many of us are so busy, as if we are caught in a race. Either we aim for one of the 'prizes' (whichever one we aim for) or we hope to rush just busily enough not to be one of the last and risk getting left behind. Once we start comparing with our peers, we feel anxious about a need to attain a certain status — be it a desirable career, title, car or house. As we wonder if we are running the rat race, do we risk losing our sense of purpose?

This anxiety spills over to education. For our concern over our children's & students' grades, the quick fix is to pack in more tutoring, which may result in over-scheduling and burnout. Never mind, at least for now, that the pressure to perform can suffocate any genuine motivation to learn the subject. As parents or educators, we feel a need to succeed in our roles to help our younger generation achieve the best possible results, outperform in a range of activities from sports to the arts, and get admitted into the top schools. How else can we measure, or display, our 'success'?

Or we become disengaged from real people. We are so hooked to our phones, computers, gaming devices or an addiction that we are too embarrassed to acknowledge.

In the midst of all these, do we drift away from each other and lose touch with the people whom we should care about?

On a community and global level, there are other worrisome trends:

- As we marvel at the pace of technological progress, we also see more people are getting stressed by fast-paced changes and increasing competition. Artificial Intelligence (A.I.) and smarter robots threaten to make more jobs obsolete.

- Increasing cases of cheating, break-ups, and outbursts of conflict among groups of people with differing ideologies.

- We bemoan the loss of our tradition and cultural heritage either to modernisation or foreign influences.

- Greed and overconsumption that stem from our unsustainable lifestyles have led to irreversible degradation of our environment and climate change.

Of the great civilisations of the past, many of them collapse due to the society's inability to respond to the degradation of the environment or social relationships.[1] Our civilisation faces the same risks today.

This book is also about the interconnection of values to garden and nature. Healthy gardens and waterways attract beautiful butterflies, birds, bees, damselflies and dragonflies.[2] Similarly, what we attract to our lives is a reflection of the state of our inner being.

The cautious optimists in us believe that there has to be a more uplifting way. We see hope in a quiet approach through nature and values that can help us thrive and remain rooted to what is truly worthwhile.

"Life is never made unbearable by circumstances, but only by lack of meaning and purpose," noted Dr. Viktor Frankl, a renowned psychiatrist and Second World War Holocaust survivor.

Living according to a set of well-chosen values and being in harmony with nature can help us find our inner motivation, meaning and purpose. Back in the days of ancient Greece, wise people had recommended the cultivation of 'arete', a Greek word which can be translated as 'excellence' or 'moral virtue'.

The measure of our lives is not just the sum total of our 'A' grades, medals, awards and promotions that are won by being superior to other people. Beyond that, our lives find deeper fulfilment through *joyful connections*, *overcoming adversity*, and a *life of meaningful contributions*. In particular, contributions to causes that are bigger than ourselves.

On some days, we feel our imperfect selves are unworthy to write about such a lofty topic; but we also have days where we boil over with enthusiasm, eager to share our findings. The following pages lay out a sequence of questions that we have found useful, show our attempts to answer them, and share our case example of the values & plants we have chosen to cherish or cultivate.

We hope our nature-inspired way will spark our readers' interest to embark on a fulfilling journey with their team/family members — to support each other to contribute purposefully and to become better people through cultivating well-chosen values. What a special opportunity indeed in the few precious years we have with them!

Our Garden Path

Does Beauty Serve a Purpose?

1

> *"Flowers are beautiful hieroglyphics of nature,*
> *with which she indicates how much she loves us."*
> — JOHANN WOLFGANG VON GOETHE

Call it love at first sight.

The first thing that draws us into the world of plants is the beauty of its flowers — their captivating colours, elegance and mesmerising patterns of petals.

Flowers with three or five petals are commonly seen. The number of petals on many species of flowers usually follow a certain pattern: either 2, 3, 5, 8, 13, 21, 34, 55, 89 petals and so on, although there are exceptions. The next number in the sequence is the sum of the previous two numbers (for example, 2+3 = 5 and 34+55 = 89). Nature indeed plays with mathematics![3]

When leaves grow on a plant, the arrangement of the leaves is in a spiral around the plant stem, in a surprisingly mathematical order. This occurs to pack in more leaves around the stem and spread them in order not to shield too much sunlight from the leaves below.[4]

From the plant's design, such arrangements increase its likelihood of survival and flourishing. From the human point of view, we see beauty. We seem to appreciate the beauty of those natural features that maximises the well-being of living things.

When we love nature back, we spend unhurried time with it. As we start to appreciate more deeply, we see more than just external beauty. Some species are edible, many are fragrant, and many more are useful. Their sweetness attract delightful butterflies to them. We are also drawn to these features of their inner beauty.

The patterns and qualities that maximises the species' likelihood of survival (and thriving) seem to be perceived as the most alluring.

Charming colours[5] : Nature helps us to reduce stress, improve the performance of our working memory and help us form new ideas.[6]

We believe nature can help us in another important way — to become better people by connecting us to our values.

Values encompasses moral virtues and character strengths; they can also be understood more broadly as a set of 'excellences', or desirable qualities that help oneself and others to thrive. The equivalent phrase in the Chinese language is 'mei-de' (美德) — the first word 'mei' means beauty or good. When people exercise good values, we perceive a sense of beauty about them, and our inner beings feel elevated.

Speaking of beauty — instead of judging people by how good they look externally, the clothes they wear, their skin colour or language they speak, we are encouraged to look deeper — into who they really are. Their inner beauty. We can only see the kinds of beauty that we have or are ready to cultivate, because we see others not as they are, but as we are.

This means we ought to look deeper into who we really are. Even as imperfect as we are, what inner beauty do we possess?

 **REFLECTION**

Which kinds of inner beauty do we appreciate in ourselves and in others?

....

....

....

....

....

....

....

....

> *"If only our eyes saw souls instead of bodies,*
> *how very different our ideals of beauty would be."*
> — ANONYMOUS

🌿 *Simpoh Air[7], usually found near the water's edge, is a native plant of Southeast Asia. Birds eat the red seeds in the star-shaped fruit.*

How Shall We Choose Our Values?

For thousands of years, civilisations have relied on the wisdom of good values to guide our lives.

Take for instance, the Aesop's fables. Aesop was a slave and storyteller who lived in Greece more than 2500 years ago. His moral lessons continue to resonate today. We are familiar with stories such as the hare and the tortoise: "slow and steady wins the race". Consider a somewhat similar meaning from a different culture in Asia: in the Malay/Indonesian proverb, *"sedikit demi sedikit, lama lama menjadi bukit"* means bit by bit, eventually a hill is formed.

Values that are well chosen, upon closer examination, should increase the chances of the survival of our species, biodiversity and improve the well-being of our globally inter-connected communities. Professor Jared Diamond, a distinguished geographer and scientist, campaigned for the need to reappraise values: "Perhaps the crux of success or failure of a society is to know *which values to hold onto*, and *which ones to discard* and *replace with new values, when times change.*"[8]

One valuable cultural heritage is the eastern philosophy on the cultivation of virtues. One ancient phrase that makes a lasting impression on us is that the wise and virtuous take delight in *water* and *mountain*.[9] Both are essential elements in Chinese and Korean landscape paintings, as well as in Japanese dry landscape gardens (枯山水, pronounced in Japanese as kare-sansui, which means dry portrayal of mountain and water).

We can view our values from these two perspectives:

Water, which represents the *source* of life

Mountain peaks, which represent our *aspirations*.

We explore each of these perspectives in more detail.

Dry landscape gardens are famous in Kyoto. Mountains surrounded by the sea are represented by the bigger rocks among a spread of smaller pebbles.[10] The garden is a paragon of simplicity: the only plant in the garden is the moss next to the bigger rocks. Apple's Steve Jobs was said to have drawn inspiration from these gardens for his minimalist approach to design.

Source Values:
How Do We Contribute?

Water is the source of life. A flowing stream, river, lake or sea contributes to the sustenance of life. Most of the major civilizations have been founded on the banks of major rivers, such as the Nile, Tigris-Euphrates, Indus, Yangtze, Mekong and the Mississippi, or along lakes and seashores such as the Mediterranean Sea. Even in modern times, when scientists scan for signs of life on other planets or moons, one of the first things they look for is the presence of water.

Behaviours and frequent actions that reflect the values that tap into our source of who we are, that naturally flows from our core and that we contribute from — is like water. We feel more *in the flow* and spontaneous when we contribute from within our source.

When we peer closer at our contributions or achievements, typically we find the blossoming of our talents that are aligned with our source values.

REFLECTION

In my family, school or organisation, which words come to mind when the team members are asked to describe my best self?

I'm someone who is...

☺ ....   ☺ ....

☺ ....   ☺ ....

☺ ....   ☺ ....

Aspirational Values:
What Kind of People Do We Choose to Become?

On the other hand, the values that we desire, that we put our energy to strive for, are our aspirational values — it's like ascending a mountain. For centuries, the peaks of the mountains have been regarded as the places to encounter the divine. These are the higher places that we aspire to.

These values, based on our aspirations of certain desired excellences, can be adopted without concern for the criticism that we still fall short of achieving the ideals — this is a recognition that we are still a 'work-in-progress'.

From our experience, source values are easier for the team members to agree upon due to a familiarity or mastery of skills related to the value. For example, 'vitality' as a value was readily adopted in our team because we are already exercising regularly.

In contrast, our team took many weeks of discussion to understand the practical implication of what the proposed aspirational values mean in our day-to-day life before there was going to be a willing adoption, a buy-in. When we commit to the aspirational value, we start to have new ideas of what suitable activities to pursue.

Choosing aspirational values do not need to be based on what is easy to achieve or the abilities we may possess. In the famous Harry Potter story, Professor Albus Dumbledore gave this advice to Harry, "It is our choices that show us what we truly are, far more than our abilities."[11]

Our choices reflect what we value most in our lives.

> REFLECTION
> Which qualities do we admire and aspire to have?

What is Our Identity?

Taken together, source values and aspirational values can help define our identity. An identity based on a carefully chosen set of 'excellences'.

Another observation about identity. Native plants are well adapted to the local environment and weather. They are also uniquely adapted to contribute to the ecosystem by providing shelter and food to specific species of birds, insects and other animals of that region. We are proud of our native plants — during our walks in nature along the water's edge, we stop by the *Simpoh Air* to appreciate its yellow flowers and pink flower-shaped fruits.

The same can be said about our local values and traditions. We feel comfortable in our own skin. Each ethnic group can feel proud of its own colour, language and cultural heritage. We celebrate the well-chosen values that have led these communities to thrive throughout the past decades and centuries.

Beliefs — Are They Compelling?

A large part of what leaders, teachers and parents do, whether consciously or not, is to shape the team members' beliefs, attitudes and preferences. These influence how we think and feel about our lives and the world around us — and have a big effect our choice of values. These values define our identity and guide our decision making.

Mahatma Gandhi, likely inspired by ancient texts, observed:

> *"Your beliefs become your thoughts.*
> *Your thoughts become your words.*
> *Your words become your actions.*
> *Your actions become your habits.*
> *Your habits become your values.*
> *Your values become your destiny."*

Our beliefs eventually lead to a set of values, which ultimately shape our life's destiny.

A compelling belief is a conviction that motivates me to act accordingly.

For aspirational values, we find that a key step is to adopt compelling beliefs. Sometimes, we fail to follow through the frequent activities, we can trace it back to beliefs that are either not very compelling, or the belief has lost its grip on our conviction.

What fills our minds and our hearts affect our beliefs. We are influenced by the media, our environment, our friends and our parents. It is worth exploring how all these influences shape our beliefs.

Our exposure to other reading and video materials around the need for conservation has led to be convinced of the need to have a more holistic perspective. This is neatly summarized by Carl Sagan, "If we are to survive, our loyalties must be broadened further, to include the whole human community, the entire planet Earth."[12] The belief led us to adopt 'wholeness' as one of our values.

REFLECTION

Think of a belief that has been influenced either by the media or the people around us. As a result, which value became a part of our lives?

What Does Our Heritage Inform Us?

A less common exercise is to explore our heritage — how our parents' ancestors pass down their beliefs through sharing or by practising their traditions. Our ancestors came from China to start life anew here. The land we live in now is multi-cultural: Malay, Indian, Chinese, Eurasian, and a diverse mix of people from all corners of the globe.

We hatched a plan for an ambitious trip: three generations took a trip back to our ancestors' hometowns in China. The entourage comprising my father, me, and Aeron (the male side) visited our old village within Putian in the province of Fujian. We, including my mother-in-law, wife, and Chloe (three generations on the female side) visited Shantou in the neighbouring Guangdong province.

My father used to wake up before dawn to release the farm animals from their pens to graze in the fields. Looking out from the old house, the newer apartments in the distance now replaced those fields.

Frugal by necessity: Re-enacting a meal of porridge and potatoes of the 1950s

After just two hours of commute on a wide expressway from the airport in Xiamen, we arrived at our ancestral village in Putian. The journey used to take many more hours along smaller roads. Even the hill where my father used to cycle up and down as a child had been flattened for the highway.

At the entrance to our ancestral house, we stood on a big slab of stone. Decades ago, several men in the family carried a big heavy block of stone for miles from a nearby hill. These stones were fashioned into slabs to be placed at the entrance of the house.

Life was difficult then. There wasn't much to eat. A typical meal consisted of watery porridge and potatoes. Scooping the porridge out into a bowl caused the sparse rice grains to swirl around the pot. Only once a year, during the Lunar New Year, the family gatherings would have sumptuous meals with meat and fish.

Droughts and floods from the overflowing river were a frequent worry for my father's relatives. A search for a better life led to the migration of my grandfather and, subsequently, my father to 'nanyang' (the Chinese phrase for southern sea), now the region of Southeast Asia.

Aeron (top right) climbs the longan fruit tree[13] that his grandfather (bottom left, pointing) as a teenager used to pluck fruits for his younger brother (foreground)

In the neighbourhood, the family planted vegetables and fruit trees.

In China, plants and herbs are prized for their medicinal values for all sorts of ailments. Traditional Chinese Medicine (TCM) contains a treasure trove of knowledge linking plants to a range of health problems.

In the 1960s and 1970s, malaria was a catastrophic problem in China. A medical researcher, Madam Tu Youyou, referred to ancient TCM text which suggested an extract from the sweet wormwood plant[14]. Eventually, artimisinin, an extract from the plant, was found to be helpful to inhibit the malaria parasite. This medicine led to the survival of millions of malaria-infected people around the world! The discovery and global impact led to a Nobel Prize for Prof. Tu in 2015.

Being immersed in our own culture heritage and learning the wisdom passed down through many generations — in this case, plants — can be so enlightening. Through inter-cultural exchange, people from different races can enjoy the richness of diversity and benefit from each other's insights and wisdom passed down through the centuries.

Among the many memories from this trip, the values of *hard work* and *thrift* stood out. These two values continue to be prominent in our upbringing, which continues to influence the choice of values of the second generation of immigrants.

Who Inspires Us? Why?

It is common to see people idolize famous personalities in the entertainment and sports industries, such as pop-singers, movie stars or athletes. We don't have to limit our choices to these popular options, unless they indeed live the values that we cherish.

We can visualise a fashion model who parades new clothes. We can think of a *value-model* as a different kind of model who showcases what living one or more chosen values looks like. We learn from value-models who exemplify excellence for the values that they espouse.

Our value-models do not need to be saints or be excellent in every aspect of their lives. Otherwise, we will have a hard time finding perfect role models. Many admirable people have been deficient in some aspects of their lives. This is the reason a value-model becomes our example only for the specific value or values, and is not an all-round role model for everything.

"Tell me who your heroes are and I'll tell you how you'll turn out to be. The qualities of the one you admire are the traits that you, with a little practice, can make your own, and that, if practiced, will become habit forming," says Warren Buffett, one of the icons of the investing world widely admired for his character.

Our team's value-models come from different ethnic groups and three different continents. Some are people we know and are still alive, and some are from a bygone era. They have made vastly different types of contributions. We will elaborate about this in Chapter Four.

> **REFLECTION**
> Who are the value-models we admire? Among the people we interact with, who are living our aspirational values?

Good Values: Should We Have More?

There are many good values to choose from, unfortunately we cannot pick all of them.

Similarly, we lose focus when select too many values. Life is about choices, including choosing the values which define our identity — how we will contribute and what we aspire for. We select a small mix of source values and aspirational values carefully so as to be able to give them enough attention.

Instead of picking from a list of values, we first explore our beliefs to derive a set of values. The process to discover and reflect on our beliefs and select our values should not be rushed.

The famed Otowa waterfall[15]: Stream water supplies three water spouts, each represents a value — longevity, success (or academic success) and romantic love. Drinking from all the spouts is regarded as being greedy.

🍃 *If a place remains untended, it may be overrun with plants or trees*[16] *that we did not expect! Similarly, without consciously choosing a set of values, our lives will be shaped by external influences.*

REFLECTION
....
What are the most important beliefs that affect my life decisions?

Water lily[17]

How Does a Plant
Connect to a Value?

"To walk safely through the maze of human life, one needs the light of wisdom and the guidance of virtue."
— BUKKYO DENDO KYOKAI

Expressing and cultivating these values is like gardening or landscaping. Choosing good values that we hold dear to our heart is similar to choosing beautiful plants for our garden. Tending plants for the *outer* garden of our home or our neighbourhood becomes a metaphor for cultivating values in the *inner* garden of our lives.

Besides the aesthetic, medicinal, cultural, or historical worth, the plant world — any of the plants, flowers or trees that we choose — can help us understand values by making the abstract more concrete. Values may be too abstract to visualise. We benefit from having tangible, visible reminders of our values.

The two ways to achieve this are through the use of symbols, or more directly through analogies. The dictionary definition of analogy is a comparison of two different things based on their being alike in some way — usually there is a logical or functional similarity.

Symbolism is the use of symbols to represent an idea, such as assigning a flower or plant to represent a particular value. Unlike an analogy which requires a functional similarity, a symbol can show a less obvious connection. Usually the symbolism is the result of a historical or cultural precedent or maybe someone's imaginative association.

Take for example, the chrysanthemum: some in Australia present it as a Mother's Day gift (the flower's name ends with the letters 'mum'). In Japan, it is a royal flower. It signifies longevity and happiness. In China, chrysanthemums blooms in the cold winter air and foretells the coming of winter; the flower symbolizes adaptability.

The chrysanthemum has been regarded as one of the plants in the *Four Noble Ones* (or *Four Gentlemen*), in accordance to the Confucian view of human virtues. The plum, blossoming every cold winter, is seen as a metaphor for faithfulness and endurance. The orchid, in the spring, represents nobility, beauty and elegance. The bamboo, with summer, symbolizes uprightness, modesty, longevity and flexibility with strength. For over a thousand years, these four plants are often portrayed in Chinese paintings; the concept was later adopted in Korean and Japanese paintings.

FILL IT IN!
Which plants can we connect to our values?

Personal/Team Value   *Plant*

Useful Values for Teamwork

Common symbols in western culture: love can be represented by the rose, red tulip, blue violet, etc. There can much subjectivity in how each of us see the connection between plants and values. Or we can practise our creativity through analogy — by seeing a functional connection between values and plants.

Take for example, integrity.

Integrity can be too abstract for some to visualise. Some think of it as related to honesty. One perspective is that of 'internal consistency' or 'self-similarity, regardless of scale'[18], which can be interpreted as what we see from far is what we see up close. What we say or do that is visible by the public is the same as what we think or say to our team members, and also to ourselves. There are no significant inconsistencies.

With this interpretation, integrity shares a similar characteristic as the cauliflower and the broccoli. If we look carefully at the broccoli, it is made up of many smaller parts (florets) that appear almost identical to the bigger stalk.

Broccoli on my dinner plate. The mid-sized floret in the middle was extracted from the original/bigger floret on the left, and the smallest broccoli on the right is taken from the middle bunch.[18]

Certain species of the fern[19] also exhibit such a characteristic. If we look closely at the many smaller fronds that make up the bigger frond. If we detach one of the small fronds and view closely, it looks like the bigger frond.

> *"Look deep into nature, and you will understand everything better."*
> – ALBERT EINSTEIN

Another useful value for teamwork is 'Diversity with a Common Purpose'.

Diversity is not just about race and gender. There is diversity of ways of thinking, age (inter-generational), backgrounds and so on.

How do our personal values dovetail the team or family values? How do the team values gel with the organisational values? When we consider family teams or organisational teams, selecting and combining values well is really important. The leaders and team members agree on the core purpose and become united in the pursuit of the collective goals.

🍃 The lantana[20], with different shaped and coloured flowers, can be found abundantly in our neighbourhood. Notice the entire flower cluster and the smaller butterfly–shaped florets appear to encircle a centre. The flower arrangement of the lantana reminds us of people from diverse colours or characteristics uniting towards a core purpose.

When team members work together, conflicts are usually unavoidable. We resolve differences in opinion or approach by considering whether the issue is essential or less/non-essential.

> *"In essentials, unity;*
> *In non-essentials, liberty;*
> *In all things, charity."*
> – MARCO ANTONIO DE DOMINIS

For essential issues, the decision that reflects the unity of our team is based on our team's values that everyone agrees to uphold. For less essential issues, there can be the freedom to choose different approaches. And always remembering that the core is *charity*, as defined by Cambridge dictionary — 'the quality of being kind to people and not judging them in a severe way'.

To give a more concrete view of how we put all these elements into practice, we shall share how our inter-generational team, with a diversity of experience and perspectives, attempts to live our values.

Arabian jasmine[21]: To us, the flower's fragrance
enjoyable by all represents generosity.

Our Team's Experience

4

After evaluating our beliefs about what is important to us now and the future, and feeling inspired by several value-models, we have narrowed down our choice of values. For us, this process took more than a year.

Using our cultural tool, phrases in Chinese language and idioms, these are our three values:

(1) 创值 Co-creating Value

(2) 健全 Wholesome Vitality

(3) 朴厚 Simplicity with Generosity

值 *Value*

创 *Creativity*

朴 *Simplicity*

全 *Wholeness*

健 *Vitality*

厚 *Generosity*

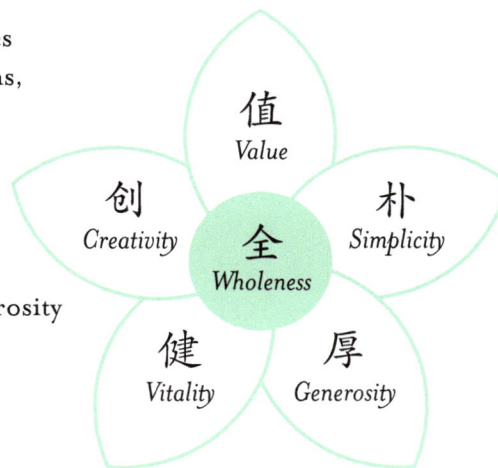

These values can be interpreted in its combined form (e.g. wholesome vitality) as well as their separate, component qualities (e.g. *vitality* as distinct from *wholesome/wholeness*).

The values of *hard work* and *thrift* passed down from our ancestors may have indirectly influenced our choice of *vitality, value/usefulness* and *simplicity.* These are the values we have updated to be more relevant to us today.

When we practise activities that represent aspirational values frequently, these values start feel more natural to us. Over time, we view certain aspirational values as more like source values. Viewed in this way, the two kinds of values are placed on two ends of a continuum.

Aspirational Values ||||||||||||||||||||||||||||||||||||||||||||||||||||||||||| *Source Values*

A decade ago, vitality was originally an aspirational value but after years of prioritising fitness, we can start to contribute through our fitness and vitality. For our team, vitality, co-creating, and value are closer to the source-value end of the continuum. Simplicity, generosity and wholeness are closer to the aspirational end.

The Importance of Personal Choice

We ought to have the internal motivation to pursue the team values. The team leader can make recommendations of the values to cultivate, but every one in the team, regardless of age or experience, has a voice to influence the choice of values to adopt.

Aeron writes: "I find these values quite good as they are chosen from my beliefs, and so I have decided to adopt these values. We try our best to have many frequent activities linked to our values, in order for these values to become source values through which we contribute. If we truly believe in our chosen set of values, we would be motivated to follow it and live our lives according to it."

Notwithstanding her own independent mind, Chloe agrees, "I want to do more things related to our values."

(Note: Other teams and families with different set of beliefs and preferences may arrive at a different set of values).

The clove[22] is a precious spice exported from Southeast Asia to other continents since the middle ages. It can be a symbol for value or usefulness. 'The Clove' tree sculpture is a collaboration between Titus Yong and Argentinian artist Joaquín Fargas.

✿ Co-creating Value

Our choice of Plant as a Symbol for this value:

Hybrid Orchid

An orchid hybrid created for animal scientist Jane Goodall[23]. The hybrid was a result of cross–pollination between two orchid species. She took a calculated risk to go from England to Tanzania in order to research on chimpanzees.

The outer garden plant that is an analogy for 'co-creating' is the hybrid orchid. The hybrid orchid is produced by cross breeding two different species of orchids. This mirrors the way that creativity happens, which is when two different ideas are combined.

Chloe loves hybridizing orchids. She finds removing the cap from the anther to gather the pollen, then pollinating the sticky stigma a very fun activity.

Our compelling beliefs that support co-creating value:

- Deep, social relationships is the foundation for well-being. Co-creating something of lasting value is a meaningful way to spend time together.

- Co-creating value will enlarge the pie, and help us create new lunch dishes together!

- Creativity is a skill that gets better with practice.

Our value-models:

- Studio Ghibli, co-founded by Miyazaki Hayao and Takahata Isao. The studio created the much loved animations such as *My Neighbour Totoro, Spirited Away,* and *Princess Mononoke* (which deals with the theme of environmental destruction).

- Wilbur and Orville Wright, the brothers who were the first to design and fly an aeroplane in 1903. Instead of fighting as siblings typically do, they focused on co-creating value.

- Sun Yu-li, a leading Asian sculptor, is a model for several of our values such as creativity, simplicity and wholeness.

Our frequent activities for co-creating value:

- Have fun trying new, adventurous things and be willing to take calculated risks. This includes writing this book together.

- Practice observation skills and recording ideas that solve problems.

- Go for walks in the parks, gardens and forests to get fresh ideas.

Living the value of co-creating: Assembling our own double-decker bed

Our Story

Here's our story of risk taking, a string of failures and perseverance in our journey to co-create value:

Aeron routinely looks out for interesting ideas. One of them is an idea of a device to help school children slow down the increase in short-sightedness. Aeron and Chloe brainstormed the design, shopped for parts and experimented away. After many sets of failed prototypes pile up, frustration mounted. The likely culprit could be short circuiting or soldering problems.

The *Bhagavad Gita*, a literary gem from the Indian tradition, exhorts us to perform actions based on discipline, but not to let ourselves be too emotionally attached to the results, whether favourable or unfavourable.[24] This is especially true during experimentation, where failures abound.

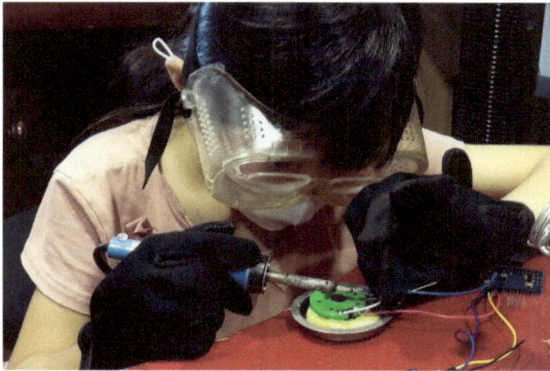

Chloe solders the wires to another electronic component.

An earlier prototype of the device. The box contains electronic components powered by a battery.

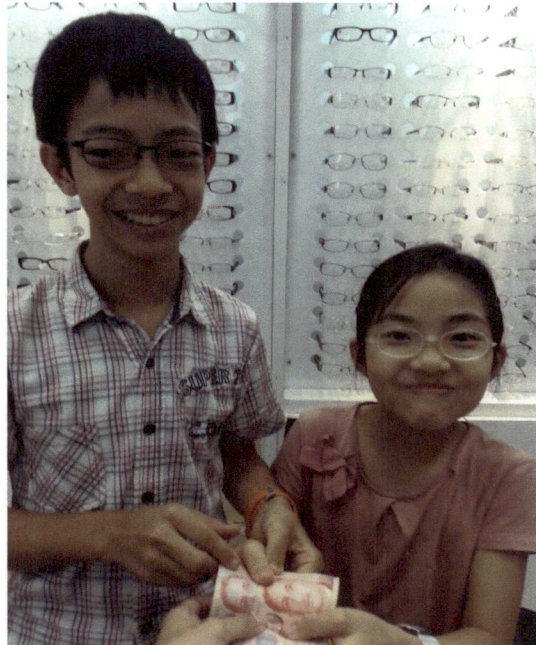

Right after a successful sales pitch! (Photo by Kellie, a new customer, as she hands over the cash payment).

✿ Wholesome Vitality

Our choice of Plant as a Symbol for this value:

Jelutong Tree

🌿 *The mighty Jelutong[25], a native tree of Southeast Asia, can grow to sixty metres tall.*

The Jelutong is a fast growing tree and fits well in the ecosystem of tropical rainforest. For us, this tree and its harmonious surrounding is a reminder of our value of 'wholesome vitality'. We visit this tree periodically at the Petai trail of MacRitchie reservoir.

For the value of 'wholesome' (and we include the related value of 'wholeness'), there is a respect for the delicate balance of our ecosystem. The dictionary definitions for *vitality* include: 'life force', 'the state of being strong and active' and 'the power of enduring'.

Our compelling beliefs that support wholesome vitality:

- A fit body leads to a sharp mind.

- Our contributions are cumulative over our lifetimes. We prioritize activities that enable long, productive lives over short-term results.

- "If we are to survive, our loyalties must be broadened further, to include the whole human community, the entire planet Earth." — Carl Sagan

Our frequent activities for wholesome vitality:

- Regular exercise and getting enough sleep. Our exercises include a range of activities done for fun and serious training. In training for sports, we remind ourselves to prioritize improving on our collective best times over beating competitors.

- Eating more fruits and vegetables & drinking enough water regularly.

- Taking walks in nature: gardens, reservoirs and forests. Cherish our trees for providing oxygen for the fresh air we breathe.

Our value-models:

🍃 Haile Gebrselassie: Ethiopian running legend who set twenty seven world records. After his last race, he said: "I'm retiring from competitive running, not from running. You cannot stop running, this is my life".[26]

🍃 Wangari Maathai: Kenyan environmentalist, founder of the Green Belt Movement, the first African female to be conferred the Nobel Peace Prize. To help poor, rural Kenyan women, she led a movement that eventually planted over fifty millions of trees. These trees supplies a host of materials that improve the quality of life of many Africans.

🍃 Felix Finkbeiner: Felix, as a nine-year-old in 2007 and inspired by Wangari Maathai, hatched a plan to plant one million trees in his home country of Germany. Now, as a teenager, his organisation, Plant-for-the-Planet, together with United Nation's Billion Tree campaign, has planted more than fourteen billion trees in 130 countries. The National Geographic reported that the initiative he started is on track to plant a trillion trees.[27] Even an inexperienced youth can start to become a force for positive change.

Most of the time, practising our values are just ordinary, unremarkable events. But we can still make our little moments more memorable.

Jumping for joy! Greeting the aeroplane after cycling to East Coast Park.

Forest immersion on the Rock Path, Bukit Timah Nature Reserve

Occasionally, one gets to experience a peak experience. Aeron was delighted to be invited to perform in the finale of Chingay 2015, an annual street performance. Years of training and weeks of on-site practice equipped him for this challenging task to entertain tens of thousands of spectators.

Aeron climbs the 50-metre (16-storey) sky ladder above the 'Tree of Hope' parade float at the Chingay finale performance

✿ Simplicity with Generosity

Our choice of Plant as a Symbol for this value:

Frangipani

🍃 *The frangipani flowers appear in abundance in our neighbourhood. In the mornings, on our way out of our house, we often see many frangipani flowers, some fallen to the ground.*

The frangipani[28], mostly plain white and fragrant, is our pick for *simplicity with generosity*. Often planted at temple grounds and used in funerals, the frangipani reminds us of our brief lives and to focus on what is truly important.

In a survey initiated by the Harvard Graduate School of Education, ten thousand youth from different races were asked to prioritize three items.[29] Around 80% of those surveyed chose personal *accomplishments* or *happiness*. Only around 20% prioritize *caring for others*. It should not come as a surprise that increasingly more people question if capitalism works anymore. Most of us prioritize succeeding and being happy first, and then, maybe, those who have succeeded will give back to society.

Simplicity with generosity may not have been our natural choice. The society's dominant concept of success is material riches and luxury. For a large part of our lives, we have been concerned mostly about ourselves. We look back at some of our inconsiderate behaviours and wished we had acted differently.

We debated about the implication of this combined value — are we choosing to deprive ourselves of nice things? Do we have to give away most of our things? Will we be taken advantage of? We do not yet have clear answers on where to draw the line, but we are willing to pick this value because we cherish the idea of the kind of people we will become.

Simplicity and generosity seems to be a good way to control greed. If we live simply and are willing to share with others, wouldn't this reduce the likelihood of dishonesty?

Our compelling beliefs that support simplicity with generosity:

❧ Living a simple life is our way of showing gratitude to mother earth.

❧ If we are generous to others first, the universe will be generous to us.

❧ Simplicity with Generosity is the mirror of the beautiful soul.

Our value-models:

We admire two contrasting figures, Mahatma Gandhi and Warren Buffett.

૪   Gandhi lived a minimalist life with few belongings. He was generous to dedicate his life to pursue a worthy cause for his countrymen.

૪   Warren Buffett, despite being one of the richest billionaires, still lives frugally. Instead of splurging on an extravagant life, he generously donated a large part of his wealth to the foundation run by his friends, Bill and Melinda Gates. Mr. Buffet recalls that his teacher Benjamin Graham had hoped "to do something foolish, something creative, and something generous" every day. We view this as an encouragement to take ourselves less seriously, do something fun or whimsical, and laugh at ourselves!

Our frequent activities for simplicity with generosity:

૪   We refrain from buying things that we do not need. We learn to share things with our neighbours and relatives. If we live a simpler life, we will have less carbon footprint and help save the environment. If we have too many unnecessary items, our lives will be cluttered. Keep only the essential items.

૪   Practising gratitude. Recognizing how fortunate our lives have been and being grateful for our circumstances is a powerful motivator for generosity.

૪   Practising *Kind Deed for the Day* (in short, we call it KDD). "Charity begins at home": we can start by doing a small chore for a family member. Eventually we can extend this deed to a friend, or even a stranger!

Our Story

Practising small but frequent activities is an easier way for newbies like us to get started.

Once, we tried a bolder idea. Aeron, Chloe and their friends discussed ways to raise money for underserved children. They roped in their classmates to sell used and new items next to their school canteen. Together they donate their seldom-used or new items for the sale. Reducing items for a simpler life and yet benefiting others. That's achieving two objectives with one initiative.

As we discover more about the benevolent side of humanity, we learnt that there are better ways to do our part as citizens of this fragile world. We will explore how to improve and sustain worthwhile initiatives.

Mini fund-raising effort: People show a higher degree of motivation if they volunteer for the task.

For aspirational values, how else shall we begin? We use our more familiar source values to bridge the gap — by combining source and aspirational values. Below are two examples, showing varying degrees of success:

(1) *Generosity* combined with *vitality*:

We organised a climbing activity with students in our neighbourhood to help them appreciate about fitness and think about their aspirations.

Nineteen students, including a six-year-old and many who seldom exercise, managed to climb fifty storeys to the top! Such is the power of mutual encouragement.

(2) *Simplicity* combined with *wholeness* and *vitality*:

We learn to cook vegetarian food and aim to eat less meat. Chloe wrote: "We eat vegetarian meals that are simple. I feel that simplicity is needed to reduce our carbon footprint."

Cooking experiment: can we choose healthier ingredients?

One day, while we were eating our vegetarian dinner, Chloe blurted, "I don't really believe in this vegetarian thing anymore. It's so inconvenient. Everywhere we go, there are so few choices." She was referring to the school canteens and inexpensive food courts. Or maybe meat tastes better?

Under such circumstances, our beliefs can be fragile. Our beliefs could not withstand such inconveniences or long-standing preferences. We need to revisit why some of our beliefs have felt less compelling, be inspired all over again by our value-models and cherish the plant that represent the value. We shall also take time to learn to cook more delicious vegetarian meals. This can be an ongoing process for each of the affected values.

Simplicity with generosity, as our aspirational value, doesn't occur so naturally yet. Being around with people who live this value should help inspire us to practise these values more often.

Tulips in Butchart Gardens[30]

Cultivating Values

Savour Our Vegetables

Every type of healthy diet recommended by nutritionists and doctors are big on vegetables, fruits, whole grains and nuts. The cauliflower and the broccoli, which we described earlier as our symbols for integrity, are vegetables commonly cited as providing a number of health benefits.

Eating vegetables is a more sustainable way of living compared to eating mostly meat. Due to the way animals are reared for food, producing each kilogram of meat takes much more resources than for each kilogram of vegetables. A quick comparison of the average amount of water to produce a kilogram of food item: Beef (15,500 litres!), chicken (3,900 litres), orange (460 litres), cabbage (200 litres).[31]

At times, as we eat a vegetable, we playfully imagine that the value symbolized by it can become digested and absorbed into our bloodstream. What a fantastic way to assimilate a value in our lives, if only it were that simple! Nevertheless, savouring our vegetables, bite by bite, is a reminder to practise those values, bit by bit, to grow our inner selves.

> **QUICK THOUGHT**
> Which vegetables could we eat more often?

Cherish our Trees

When we visit the trees that embody our values, we hold an attitude of gratitude towards the trees for their silent ways of making the values more tangible for us to understand. We make it a point to visit these trees periodically and look up to them. This is one of our frequent activities to remind ourselves what the values embody.

In one research study, participants who stood in a grove of towering trees felt a sense of awe — they subsequently showed increased helping behaviour and decreased feeling of entitlement (a reduced sense of self-importance relative to something larger).[32]

Being in the forest and soaking up the air around the old trees is a practice known as 'forest immersion' or 'forest bathing'[33]. Walking in the woods without using our phones can reduce one's stress. The air contains a certain chemical called phytoncides, which is found in the essential oils of wood, plants and certain vegetables and fruit. Trees emit this to protect themselves from certain insects and germs; for humans, the effect of this increases our body's natural killer cells which improves the immune system function. This natural aromatherapy is claimed to be the medicine of being in the forest.

> MAKE A LIST
> Where is a convenient woody area that we can visit? This can be a cluster or line of trees in my neighbourhood or a forest.
>
> 🌲 1.
>
> 🌲 🌲 2.
>
> 🌲 🌲 🌲 3.

Cherish nature by taking hikes into the woods and appreciating its biodiversity. Chloe savours being immersed in a montane forest on Mt. Brinchang in Malaysia.

Cultivate our Gardens

We can also cherish nature by nurturing plants or cultivating a garden.

*Chloe's terrarium in our home garden is a simple way to start a
mini garden. As we get more proficient with it, we can add more
plants or expand our garden to other parts of our home.*

Think of the terrarium as a space capsule. For humans to survive long space trips to other habitable planets on other galaxies, we need to grow our own food in a tight space and keeping our plants alive. This is long-term holistic thinking. Ensuring the future survival of mankind involves cultivating the right plants.

Nurturing the plant takes patience, the same goes for cultivating a value. Tending to growing seeds is a great way to learn patience. Plants operate in cycles of days, weeks or months, not in computer mouse clicks or download speeds. We can cultivate a garden within our house or near our house compound in designated community areas.

Planting a garden involves understanding the conditions for it to thrive such as sunlight, water, fertilizer and seasons. Cultivating values is like cultivating a garden. It involves choosing the seeds or graft, and carefully providing the conditions for the plant to grow. We practise the frequent activities suited to the values. Some plants prefer an exposure to the sun, some partial exposure, some require more water than others. The same apply for the values — we need to tailor the types and frequency of activities that cultivate them.

Consider the proportion of time we spend in activities that are in line with our values with what we deem as most important. That tells us whether we are on our way to becoming the person we aspire to be.

Our frequent activities, not what we say, are the true measures of what we value. Some frequent activities can turn into habits: as creatures of habit, we eventually become who we practise to be.

REFLECTION
Which activities should we start doing today? How can we make it more likely to practise those activities more frequently?

Ideas for Action

We hope our readers will be inspired to cultivate our outer garden of plants as a reminder to cultivate our inner garden of values.

Here is a summary of the seven action items. If any of them resonate with you, please feel free to adopt them:

1. Reflect on our beliefs and preferences. Select a combination of source values and aspirational values that help us grow into the kind of persons we want to become.

2. Choose our value-models wisely. Their life examples teach us what living the values mean.

3. Select the vegetables, flowers, plants or trees that represent our values. Let these symbols serve as frequent reminders to cultivate our values.

4. Eat more vegetables, fruits, whole grains and nuts regularly. Be mindful of the values we are putting into our beings daily.

5. Cultivate a small garden with the chosen plants. Decide which types of activities and practices will support and fulfil these values. Schedule these activities into our lives; practise them frequently.

6. Take strolls periodically in the woods and gardens to cherish the shrubs and trees. Adopt an attitude of awe and gratitude to these trees for being the lungs of our earth and for symbolizing our chosen values.

Get Connected with Our Community!

7. Support each other in the nature-inspired way towards becoming better people and more fulfilling teams.

❧ Sign up for email updates at our website: www.gardenofvalues.com

❧ Facebook: Garden of Values

❧ Write to us: hello@gardenofvalues.com

> *"We may think we are nurturing our garden,*
> *but of course it's our garden that is really nurturing us."*
> — JENNY UGLOW

Hearts of caring

Hanging Lobster Claw[34]

Credits

A special shout out to Jia Lee for her wonderful graphical layout, feedback and cover illustration.

Our heartfelt thanks to the people who have provided generous support or assistance: Quek Ser Aik, Heng Swee Kiang, Parveen Singh, Nadine Yap, Mary Ha Loehr, AC Ho, Kellie Tan, Sheryl Koh, Sophie Bochot, Tay Sook Muay, Janice Lua, Sarah-Jane Tan, Stephanie Tahiri, Carolyn Tan, Sun Yu-li, Nah Juay Hng, Chi Hailu, Hidayah Amin, Nidhi Goenka, Masuda Eriko, Sudhir Thomas Vadaketh, and many others whom we may have inadvertently omitted.

We appreciate the efforts of our parents and parents-in-law to keep our cultural heritage alive and for passing on values that have been useful.

Many thanks to our wonderful teachers who have guided us well.

We are thankful to Lee Ching, as a supportive wife and mother of this family-team, for living these values together, and contributing photos and feedback. And the long-suffering love despite our failings while trying to get this project right.

I am grateful to my two children, Chloe and Aeron, who had contributed (using their lives) to the case example in this book, spending the bulk of their holidays taking thousands of photos for this project, and researching on plants & values.

And, not forgetting this project's impetus — Chloe's love for plants.

References

Introduction

1.   Diamond, Jared (2005). *Collapse: How Societies Choose to Fail or Succeed.*
      Prologue pp. 21— 24, Viking Press.
      The five factors for the collapse of past civilisations: (1) damage to
      the environment, (2) climate change, (3) hostile neighbours, (4)
      decreased support by friendly neighbours, and/or (5) a failure by
      the society to adapt to those changing circumstances.

2.   Common parasol dragonfly (*Neurothemis fluctuans*) perched on a grass.

Chapter 1

3.   The 1,1,2,3.5,8... sequence is known as the Fibonacci numbers.
      https://www.sciencenews.org/article/mathematical-lives-plants

4.   The spiral in leaves on a stalk corresponds to the golden ratio
      optimises the number of leaves and amount of sunlight each leaves
      gets for photosynthesis. The study of plant pattern formation or
      leaf arrangement is known as phyllotaxis.
      http://www.math.smith.edu/phyllo/

5.   Autumn colours by the Swift river, White Mountain National
      Forest, New Hampshire, USA.

6.   Tyrväinen, L, et al. The influence of urban green environments
      on stress relief measures: A field experiment, *Journal of Environmental
      Psychology*, Vol. 38, June 2014, p. 1— 9.

      Bratman, G.N., et.al. The benefits of nature experience: Improved
      affect and cognition, *Landscape and Urban Planning*, Volume 138, June
      2015, p. 41—50.

Chapter 2

7. Simpoh Air (*Dillenia suffrusticosa*), Chemperai trail, MacRitchie reservoir. This flower of this specie is the national flower of the country of Brunei.

8. Diamond, Jared (2005). *Collapse: How Societies Choose to Fail or Succeed.* Chapter 15: p. 443, Viking Press.

9. Excerpt from *The Analects of Confucius.* 《论语》 6.23: 智者乐水，仁者乐山 (read as: zhì zhě yuè shuǐ, rén zhě yuè shān). Translation: The wise takes delight in the water, the benevolent in mountains.

10. Ryōan-ji rock garden, northwest Kyoto, Japan.

11. Rowling, J.K. (1998). *Harry Potter and the Chamber of Secrets.*

12. Sagan, Carl (1980). *Cosmos.* Random House, New York

13. Longan tree (*Dimocarpus longan*) in Putien, Fujian province, China.

14. Sweet wormwood plant (*Artimisia annua*), native to Asian regions. Chinese name: 青蒿 (read as: qīnghāo)

15. The Otowa waterfall at the Kiyomizu-dera (清水寺), which means 'Pure Water Temple', a UNESCO World Heritage Site in Kyoto. People near and far come to queue for a drink from its waters.

16. Ancient temple intermingle with tree (likely to be *Tetrameles nudiflora*). Location: Ta Prohm, Angkor, Siem Reap province, Cambodia.

Chapter 3

17. Water lily (*Nymphaea sp.*), outside ArtScience Museum.

18. Broccoli (*Brassica oleracea* var. *italica*) exhibits some properties of the fractal, in which similar patterns recur at progressively smaller scales.
http://rationalwiki.org/wiki/Integrity
https://www.scientificamerican.com/gallery/fractals-in-broccoli/

19. Fern species such as the rabbit's foot fern (*Davallia denticulata*), white rabbit's foot fern (*Davallia teyermannii*), giant brake fern (*Pteris tripartita*).

20. Lantana (*Lantana camara* cultivars)

Chapter 4

21. Arabian jasmine (*Jasminum sambac*) at the Fragrant Garden, Singapore Botanic Gardens. It is the national flower of the Philippines (locally known as *sampaguita*) and one of the three national flowers of Indonesia (*melati putih* in Indonesian). It is used for making perfume and jasmine tea.

22. Clove, the aromatic flower bud of the clove tree (*Syzygium aromaticum*)

23. Hybrid orchid *Spathoglottis 'Jane Goodall'*, National Orchid Garden, Singapore Botanic Gardens.

24. *Bhagavad Gita* 2:48: "Perform actions, firm in discipline, relinquishing attachment; be impartial to failure or success."

25. Jelutong tree (*Dyera costulata*) at the Petai trail, MacRitchie Reservoir.

26. Haile Gebreselassie's retirement quote:
    http://www.bbc.com/sport/athletics/32680723

27. http://news.nationalgeographic.com/2017/03/felix-finkbeiner-
    plant-for-the-planet-one-trillion-trees/

28. Frangipani (*Plumeria rubra* cultivar) is the national flower of the
    country of Nicaragua in Central America.

29. https://mcc.gse.harvard.edu/files/gse-mcc/files/mcc-
    infographic.pdf

Chapter 5

30. Didier's tulips (*Tulipa gesneriana*), Butchart Gardens, Vancouver
    island, Canada.

31. www.waterfootprint.org/Reports/Hoekstra-2008-
    WaterfootprintFood.pdf

32. Piff, P.K., et.al. (2015). Awe, the Small Self, and Prosocial
    Behavior, *Journal of Personality and Social Psychology*, Vol. 108, No. 6, p.
    883– 899.

33. Forest bathing is known in Japanese as 森林浴 (read as: shinrin-
    yoku or in Korean as 산림욕 (read as: sanlim-yog)

    Li, Q., et.al. (2008). Visiting a forest, but not a city, increases
    human natural killer activity and expression of anti-cancer
    proteins. *International Journal of Immunopathology and Pharmacology*. Vol.
    21(1), p. 117–27.

34. Hanging lobster claw (*Heliconia rostrata*), Singapore Botanic
    Gardens.

In our modern, busy lives, do we feel overwhelmed, distracted, or a loss of a sense of meaning?

How *should* we talk to our children and teenagers about values?

Take a walk down the garden path, and guide our children to *reflect on our beliefs* and choose *excellent values*.

As a practical guide for families and educators, this book shares a refreshing way to build a desired culture.

A pleasant surprise awaits us when the transformation happens to our lives and our relationships!

ISBN 978-981-11-3631-3

9 789811 136313 >

www.ingramcontent.com/pod-product-compliance
Lightning Source LLC
Chambersburg PA
CBHW041429090426
42741CB00003B/92